Original title:
In the Heart of Christmas Light

Author: Isabella Rosemont
ISBN HARDBACK: 978-9916-94-032-7
ISBN PAPERBACK: 978-9916-94-033-4

The Warmth of Gathering Souls

A jolly crew with mismatched socks,
They share stories and homemade locks.
The cat's on a table, a sight to see,
Stealing the pie while sipping sweet tea.

Laughter erupts like pops from the pan,
Grandpa’s old jokes just won’t go as planned.
With cookies gone missing and gifts all askew,
The fun just keeps growing, all thanks to the crew.

Sparkling Memories of Frosted Cheer

Glitter strewn all over the floor,
Outfits that clash, what’s in store?
The kids are all laughing, making a mess,
While someone is caught in their grandma's dress!

Eggnog spills, and the dog dashes by,
Uncle Joe’s singing a tune, oh my!
With music and chaos, the night feels so bright,
While we toast to the moments, they fly like a kite.

Beneath the Stars of December's Eve

Frostbite on noses, but spirits are high,
Snowballs are flying like stars in the sky.
A snowman’s all dressed in last season’s flair,
With carrots from dinner, it’s quite a strange pair!

Who needs fancy gifts under the tree?
When sledding down hills feels wild and free.
A frosty mishap brings giggles and glee,
Just watch out for icicles from that old maple tree!

A Glimmer of Hope in Darkened Days

The lights twinkle bright, a sight to behold,
While a tree made of tinfoil shimmers in gold.
The jokes crackle louder than pops from the fire,
As Grandma recites tales we all surely admire.

With every bright moment, a mishap can bloom,
Like Aunt May's dance, makes the whole room go boom!
From cookies that crumble to laughter that soars,
Our hearts fill with joy, who could ask for more?

The Luminescence of Shared Smiles

Twinkling lights on every tree,
A lopsided star, oh woe is me!
The cookies burn, the cat takes flight,
Yet laughter echoes through the night.

Snowmen wobble with carrot nose,
One just fell, now who knows?
It’s a sight, oh such delight,
As we tumble in pure twilight.

Mistletoe hung with charming grace,
Uncle Bob tripped—what a race!
We’re tangled in joy, what a fright,
But all is merry, oh so bright!

As we gather 'round to cheer,
Grandma spins yarns with too much beer!
The glowing warmth within our sight,
Makes even blunders feel just right.

Woven Dreams of Hope and Light

Bows on packages, oh so tight,
Dad’s still wrapped in paper—what a sight!
Gifts are flying, not quite right,
As we giggle, hearts ignite.

The tree leans slightly, it’s a tease,
Tinsel tangled in the breeze.
Gingerbread men start a fight,
Who knew they could run so bright?

A snowball flies, it hits the cat,
Now she’s plotting, oh, how 'bout that!
Joyful chaos, a comical plight,
Yet love shines through, clear and bright.

So raise a glass to this wild night,
To merry madness, oh what a fright!
With laughter and warmth, we take flight,
In this glow, we find delight.

Echoes of Laughter in the Chill

Frosty noses and warm hands,
We dance like snowflakes in bands.
Socks mismatched, a humorous sight,
We chuckle and twirl in pure delight.

Gingerbread men run for their lives,
With icing smiles, they try to survive.
Cookies hidden, a sneaky delight,
We nibble and giggle throughout the night.

Illuminated Paths of Love

Balloons of joy float in the air,
As we trip and stumble without a care.
Laughter echoes from rooftop to street,
While elves make mischief on tiny feet.

Wreaths gone rogue, swinging in glee,
Cats in Santa hats climb up a tree.
With giggles around, it’s a sight so bright,
Even the snowmen join in the flight.

The Enchantment of a Thousand Lights

Twinkling bulbs make us squint and stare,
Tangled lights? Why do we still dare?
Decorations dancing, a comical show,
Doodles and sparkles, all aglow.

Sleigh bells jingle, a tune out of tune,
Fuzzy socks prance to the light of the moon.
Mittens mismatched, a fashion faux pas,
Yet we strut our stuff with a hearty hurrah.

Celestial Wishes on the Snow

Stars sprinkle wishes down from above,
While we try to catch them, what a shove!
Snowballs fly with a mischievous cheer,
As laughter erupts, spread far and near.

Chubby cheeks and laughter abound,
With penguins sliding all over town.
We’ll raise a toast to the clumsy and bright,
As we roll in the snow, hearts light as a kite.

Festive Spirits Among Whispering Pines

Pine trees shaking, looking spry,
Elves in tights and reindeer fly.
Snowflakes tickle noses bright,
Giggling kids in pure delight.

Cookies vanish, crumbs like fate,
Santa stuck, oh, what a weight!
Chimneys breathing smoke so warm,
Jingle bells now sound the alarm!

A Canvas of Lights in the Winter Sky

Twinkling bulbs on rooftops high,
Squirrels skirmish, oh my, oh my!
Snowmen dance with carrots bold,
Frosty tales of laughs retold.

Neighbors fuss, they hang the wreath,
One cat claws through, like a thief.
Hats go flying, laughter swells,
Underneath the ringing bells!

The Softness of Dreams on Christmas Eve

Blankets soft as clouds at night,
Dreaming of the cookie bite.
Rudolph's nose, a beacon bright,
Caution, kids, don’t cause a fright!

Socks are hung with bated breath,
Hoping for a toy, not death.
Santa’s sleigh, now where’s that thing?
Off the roof—what joy it brings!

Heartstrings Tied with Ribboned Light

Tangled lights, oh what a mess,
Yelling “Help!”—who will digress?
Presents wrapped with love and flair,
Tape disasters fill the air.

Mittens lost, we've looked for days,
Frogs in boots jump through the haze.
Giggles bounce like bells that chime,
Funny moments, oh so sublime!

Luminal Pathways to Togetherness

Candles flicker, shadows dance,
Grandma’s cookies, a sugary trance.
Uncle Joe rhymes with a twist,
Laughter bursts, we can't resist.

Lights are tangled in the halls,
Dancing ornaments, they take falls.
Squeaky reindeer hooves on the roof,
Whispers of joy, that's the proof.

Wrapped in paper, giggles so loud,
Presents unbox, we feel so proud.
Cats in trees, what a delight,
Hiding gifts from each other’s sight.

Holiday sweaters, too bright to wear,
Family photos, we can't compare.
Snowflakes swirl, we build a man,
With a carrot nose, oh what a plan!

Traces of Joy in Frosty Air

Nose to nose, frost on the glass,
Kids throw snowballs, hoping they'll pass.
Giggling friends take a quick spill,
Hot cocoa warms, yet gives a chill.

Sledding down hills, screams fill the sky,
Socks all mismatched, oh my oh my!
Elves in pajamas, all in a row,
Chasing brown dogs who steal the show.

Wrapped in scarves, colors so bright,
Rudolph's red nose is shining tonight.
Chickens in hats, a sight to behold,
As carolers sing tales of the bold.

Word got out of the cookie stash,
Santa's on diet; we'll verify that bash.
Eggnog spills on the best of dress,
A festive mess that we must confess!

The Glow of Heartfelt Gatherings

Chimney smoke curls in the air,
Pies in the oven, a festive flare.
Turkey bumbles, it's quite the fuss,
Grandpa snores; we quietly discuss.

Laughter spills like the mulled wine,
Auntie's secret, what's in that brine?
Kids at the table, stories they weave,
All share a laugh 'til we can't believe.

Lights blinking wildly, more like a show,
The cat in the tree puts on a glow.
Players in pajamas, we're cozy and neat,
Dancing to tunes from a jukebox beat.

Joining hands, we harmonize,
A chorus of mishaps, our feelings arise.
Gifts wrapped in giggles, surprises in tow,
Togetherness shines, with room for more glow!

Holiday Magic Beneath the Treetops

Under the twinkling, tangled lights,
Elves on the mantle, having fun fights.
Dogs with reindeer horns, what a sight,
Presents piled high, oh what a night.

Candy canes hang from every branch,
Join in the fun, everyone’s got a chance.
A smooth tune plays, we all take a twirl,
Sisters in slippers, giving a whirl.

Jokes about socks, the gifts that we dread,
Who'll get the sweater that looks like Fred?
Tinsel rain falls as we sing loud,
Creating a memory that makes us proud.

Ending the day with our hearts all aglow,
Family traditions that bring on the show.
Squeals of delight as the night starts to fade,
Holiday magic is never betrayed!

Threads of Harmony Through Time

In the kitchen, chaos reigns,
Cookies dancing, sugar chains.
A cat in a hat, what a sight,
Chasing twinkling lights at night.

Grandpa's tales, a little mistold,
Of reindeer who actually stole gold.
The tree's crooked, but who would care,
With laughter echoing everywhere.

A sweater knitted, five sizes too big,
Uncle Joe slips and does a jig.
With every giggle, memories gleam,
Threads of laughter, a holiday dream.

So raise a glass, let echoes soar,
For in this mayhem, we find much more.
With hearts entwined, we'll dance and play,
In this lovely, wild holiday sway.

Sparkling Laughter in the Winter's Breath

Snowflakes falling, a slippery tease,
Grandma's pancakes, sheer tasty breeze.
With cocoa spilled, the kids take flight,
Sledding down hills, what a glorious sight!

Presents hiding, where could they be?
Oh look, it's the dog under the tree!
With wagging tails and joyful barks,
The night unfolds like a canvas of sparks.

The neighbors sing, slightly off-key,
The carolers laugh, can you hear me?
A snowman grins with a crooked nose,
As laughter bubbles and merriment grows.

So let's embrace this frosty delight,
With steaming mugs and giggles so bright.
In winter's grip, we find our cheer,
Sparkling laughter, we hold so dear.

A Promise Written in Candlelight

Candles flicker, shadows dance,
A polka-dotted turkey in a trance.
A wish for peace hangs on the wall,
But Dad's napkin hat steals it all!

With voices raised, we sing a tune,
While cats eye the feast beneath the moon.
The dog is plotting a crafty heist,
As the pie cools, oh, let’s not be precise!

Little Timmy's speech, what a delight,
Dedicating naps as the festive rite.
With laughter shared 'round the table tight,
This promise glows under the candlelight.

So gather close, share jokes that shine,
In this cozy room, our hearts align.
The night grows old, yet smiles take flight,
With every twinkle, our spirits ignite.

The Spirit of Together in Twilight

Under the stars, we gather near,
Sipping cider, spreading cheer.
With popcorn garlands hanging low,
A cat leaps in—oh no, run for show!

Silly hats adorn our heads,
With tinsel tangled in the threads.
As stories spill like hot cocoa,
Laughter bubbles, oh what a show!

A fart joke here, a giggle there,
With silly dances, none would dare.
In cozy corners, warmth ignites,
The spirit of joy, such funny sights.

As twilight drapes its gentle cloak,
We're wrapped in love, no need for a joke.
Together we thrive, forever bright,
In this nutty world, everything feels right.

Glistening Memories of Warmth and Light

The snowman’s hat is far too wide,
He wears it with a goofy pride.
His carrot nose, a cheeky grin,
Says, "Let the games of winter begin!"

The cocoa spills when laughter reigns,
As marshmallows float like tiny trains.
We dance around, our socks all mismatched,
In this joyful chaos, our hearts are scratched.

The twinkling lights hang wild and low,
The cat’s in the tree and it’s quite the show.
With every bulb that flickers bright,
We share our tales 'til the wish of night.

So raise your cups, let moments freeze,
To every funny fall and sneeze.
This season warms, it brings delight,
And fills our hearts with sheer delight.

A Tinge of Magic in the Chill

A snowball fight goes oh-so-wrong,
With sleds that fly and cheers so strong.
I slip and slide right on my rear,
And find my friends, they're all right here.

The frost that bites, yet feels like fun,
The tumbles down till day is done.
Each breath a cloud, we giggle and prance,
In this chilly weather, we take our chance.

Our noses red, our mittens lost,
To find them now would be the cost.
Yet laughter binds like winter's cheer,
As jingle bells ring loud and clear.

With a sprinkle of love and snowflakes bright,
Magic dances in the frosty night.
So bundle up, let's make a race,
In this snowy world, we find our place.

Reflections of Love Beneath the Glow

The cookie jar is far too full,
With frosted treats that make us drool.
But as we munch, a crumbly chase,
It seems that frosting wins the race.

The tree is bright, but look—what’s that?
A squirrel’s snatched one, oh what a brat!
With lights aglow, we think we’re wise,
While playful critters claim the prize.

When all is done, the plates are bare,
We’ll share our tales, and none will care.
For laughter's love, it fills the space,
In every hug, there’s warm embrace.

So gather 'round, let jokes take flight,
We find our joy in the soft moonlight.
With hearts aglow, we raise a cheer,
To every memory that draws us near.

Twinkling Moments of Joyful Unity

The fireplace crackles, pops, and sighs,
As we unwrap gifts, oh, what a surprise!
A sweater five sizes too big for me,
Who knew Aunt May had such a spree?

The game of charades is quite a mess,
With acting skills in a state of distress.
Yet through the giggles and silly fights,
We share our bonds on these special nights.

The carols sung are off-key and loud,
Yet in this fun, we feel so proud.
With friends and family gathered here,
We note the moments that we hold dear.

Embracing quirks, we face the night,
As twinkling stars bring pure delight.
With hearts aligned, we dance in glee,
In this festive love, we're wild and free.

A Symphony of Sparkling Nights

Twinkling lights on every tree,
Dancing around quite merrily.
A cat in tinsel, what a sight,
Knocked down the cookies, oh what a plight!

Snowmen sing with carrot-nose,
Frosty jokes nobody knows.
Elf shoes squeak on the ground,
Laughter and giggles, all around!

Hot cocoa spills with marshmallow,
A sip too much? Oh, my poor fellow!
Mittens matched? Not a chance,
One's striped and one’s in a dance!

As the stars blink in the sky,
Santa's sleigh zooms by with a sigh.
What’s that? A reindeer on my roof?
Oh wait, it’s just our neighbor’s goof!

The Magic That Fills the Air

Gifts wrapped up with ribbons bright,
A dog steals one, oh what a fright!
Mom's baking cookies, flour in her hair,
Dad's stuck in the lights, it's quite the affair!

Snowflakes dance like crazy fairies,
While kids throw snowballs, not so wary.
A snowman's hat flies off in the breeze,
Heads roll over with giggles and wheeze!

Grandma's sweater, colors so bold,
She struts like a model, if truth be told.
With each little giggle, joy slinks in,
Even the cat wears a grin!

Around the tree, we break into song,
Out of tune, but we sing along.
And as the night falls with a cheer,
We trip on the twinkle lights near!

Beneath the Boughs of Hope

Under the tree, the presents stack,
But mom says, 'No peeking, that's a fact!'
Siblings sneaking, just a quick peek,
But the wrapping's so tricky, what a sneak!

Sticky fingers on the candy cane,
A taste test leads to sugar rain.
Grandpa snorts as he sips his cheer,
Spitting out eggnog—oh dear, oh dear!

Ornaments jingling, we might just scare,
The cat is plotting, with a wicked glare.
Tinsel moments, glittering and bright,
It lands on the dog, oh what a sight!

We gather close, with blankets tight,
Pillow fights erupt, what a delight!
With giggles and grumbles, we'll stay awake,
Hoping for magic on this sweet break!

Stars Beckoning through Frosted Windows

Through the frost, the stars play hide and seek,
A squirrel’s stealing from our stash, so cheek!
Neighbors carol in voices quite strange,
As the dog howls; oh, what a range!

Lights twinkle as if in a dance,
Cookies gone? Not a chance!
Santa’s sleigh parked on our roof,
Wait, it’s just our neighbor's goof!

A holiday sweater that just won’t quit,
With lights and bells, it perfectly fits.
The family gathers, yet there’s a mess,
Who left the toys? Oh, what distress!

Through frosted panes, we raise a cheer,
With laughter echoing, spreading mirth here.
As the winter wind begins to wail,
We howl right back; let's not let it fail!

Whispers of Yuletide Dreams

Jolly old Santa is stuck in the flue,
He's singing a tune and a reindeer too.
Cookies and milk were laid out with care,
But he thought it was cheese; oh, what a scare!

Elves bouncing around on their tiny little feet,
Wrapped presents in paper, oh, what a treat!
But someone misplaced sparks with gingerbread,
Now there's frosting on everything instead!

Snowmen are plotting a sneaky advance,
With carrots for noses they start the dance.
The dog is confused, thinks they're all friends,
Chasing his shadow, the fun never ends!

Frosty conspiracies bring giggles and cheer,
Laughter and joy, we hold so dear.
In this season bright, silliness reigns,
With whispers of laughter that tickle our brains.

Radiance of the Frosty Moon

A snowman in shades, rocking out at night,
Is jamming with reindeer—oh, what a sight!
Mistletoe mischief under the trees,
Kissing the air, and maybe some bees.

Gifts all around, but where's my new socks?
Found under the cat, playing with boxes!
Santa's sleigh jingles; it's stuck in the ice,
But hey, he just laughs and orders some spice.

Hot cocoa spills as we dive for the whip,
The marshmallows tumble, a sugary slip!
Snowflakes are dancing, but I can't keep pace,
Ending up sprawled with a cream-covered face!

Moonlight is twinkling over every snowdrift,
While elves on their break sip on frosty mint lift.
The magic is strong with this giggly affair,
Where laughter and joy float up in the air.

Flickering Candles in the Snow

Candles are flickering, oh what a show,
Bees are buzzing—wait, where did they go?
The cat took a swipe, it's chaos, I swear,
Now wax stains the carpet with zero to spare!

Flames dance like elves on a sugar-high spree,
While I'm trying to wrap up my gifts, can't you see?
Tinsel is tangled, the lights are a mess,
Who knew that with glue, I'd create such stress?

Gingerbread houses are leaning to one side,
While marshmallow men play slip and slide.
The dog barks at penguins made out of snow,
Chasing after us like he's ready to go!

Flickering candles light up our delight,
In this cozy chaos that feels oh-so right.
With laughter and giggles, we sing through the night,
This season brings joy; there's nothing but light!

Joyful Echoes of Silent Nights

The stockings are hung, but oh, what a fright,
They've all been raided in the depths of the night.
Gifts in disarray, such a wild little sight,
As the puppy frolics, he's filled with delight!

Mice are all dancing, dressed up in red when,
They spot that last cookie, and it's chaos again!
The tree can't stop shaking from everything found,
With squeaks and with yelps, oh, what joy abounds!

Snowflakes are swirling, the snowball fights start,
As we laugh and we giggle with pure, silly art.
The stars shine above with their twinkling grace,
While penguins in scarves waddle all over the place!

Amidst all the fun, let our laughter ignite,
In joyful echoes, our spirits take flight.
This season is magic, it's laughter we crave,
With silliness plenty and love to behave!

Enchantment in Every Glimmer

Twinkling lights dance on the floor,
Cats think it's a game, let’s explore!
Tinsel tangled in a furry guise,
Who needs a tree when there's chaos to rise?

Cookies left out, oh what a sight,
Santa’s been busy, sneaking at night!
Mouths stuffed with treats while laughter does soar,
Until the dog finds the chocolate galore!

Toys in the stockings, a lopsided cheer,
Who’d think a snowman would commandeer here?
With goggles and scarf, it’s a frosty parade,
As snowballs fly, and the kids get unmade!

So toast with cocoa, spill a bit wide,
Smiles wrapped in ribbons, we can't let it slide!
In every mishap, there's joy and delight,
As we dance through the chaos of magical night.

Joyous Shadows of Togetherness

Laughter erupts with a clattering cheer,
Grandma's surprise—now that's the real fear!
Jumping and prancing, we dodge holiday glee,
While the cat takes a nap on the tree like a spree.

Decorations are hanging, with some looking worn,
We stick on the bulbs that are slightly forlorn.
A wreath on the door, like a bird's nest askew,
Perfectly festive—or just oddly true?

Hot cocoa spills dance with marshmallows in tow,
As we all pile together for a seasonal show!
Sweaters are vintage, and fashion's a mess,
But who's counting style when there's love to profess?

So here's to the laughter, the chaos, the fun,
With family and friends, it's a race to outrun!
In shadows of warmth, the joy overstated,
We sprinkle our love—uncoordinated!

Wishes Floating on Snowflakes

Wishes carried on a frosty breeze,
Some stick to the window, to giggle or tease.
While snowmen debate a stylish new nose,
They settle for carrots, how well does it pose?

The sleds zoom past in a wobbly dance,
While mittens go missing, what happened by chance?
Hot soup makes us giggle, oh what a delight,
As cheers echo loud in this festive night.

Flakes drift down like wishes on high,
But the dog sees a squirrel and believes he can fly!
A ruckus erupts, and we laugh till we ache,
While dreams melt away like a frost-kissed cake.

So gather around for the stories retold,
With warmth in our hearts, and some memories bold.
As wishes float high on that glittery snow,
In this jolly mayhem, we happily flow.

Reflections of Warmth in Chilled Air

Chilly winds blowing through the night sky,
While cocoa-filled mugs make us giggle nearby.
Layers are piled, we resemble a drum,
With scarves flapping wide, oh, look who has come!

Candles flicker in a playful parade,
What's that? Oh dear—more pies have been made!
Whipped cream disasters and flour on faces,
Serve up the laughter, it's time for embraces!

Under the mistletoe, there's a sneaky surprise,
As grandpa leans in for a kiss, how time flies!
We snicker, we cheer while the snowflakes all fall,
Whispering secrets, love warms us all.

So toast to the small joys that come with the night,
As we share in the magic, all cozy and bright.
With reflections of laughter in this chilly affair,
We find our own warmth in the moments we share.

Flickering Hopes in the Snowy Silence

Snowflakes dance like silly sprites,
Twinkling tales of frosty nights.
Socks are stuffed with treats galore,
Will they fit? Oh, who keeps score?

Noses red and cheeks aglow,
Fumbling gift-wrap in the snow.
Kids believe in magic tricks,
While cat plays with tape, so slick!

Mittens lost by pantry door,
There's a cupcake on the floor.
I swear I put it up so high,
But look! It’s gone - oh my, oh my!

Laughter echoes, joy takes flight,
All is merry, all is bright.
Say goodbye to perfect plans,
For chaos dances in our hands.

A Journey Through Twinkling Stars

Distant twinkles, shiny sights,
Flying reindeer on snowy nights.
Santa's sleigh is missing glue,
Watch it wobble, oh, how it flew!

Cookies vanish, crumbs abound,
Rats might rob the sleigh I found.
Mighty elves with tiny boots,
Chasing cats in festive suits!

Jingle bells and silly memes,
Hearts are full, but so are dreams.
Wishing wells with socks inside,
Kid says, ‘Look! I’m Santa’s guide!’

Through the stars, we laugh and hoot,
While reindeer play their merry flute.
All the cheer, it fills the air,
Even if it needs repair!

Mysteries Wrapped in Golden Glow

Tangled lights and tangled thoughts,
Who knew stringing could be fought?
Mittens cling to mismatched pairs,
When will we clear these Christmas snares?

Wrapping paper, tape, and bows,
What’s behind this gift? Who knows!
The dog unwraps in stealthy grace,
Surprise party! What a race!

Gingerbread men take a stand,
In frosting fights across the land.
Hiding snacks from little hands,
Dreams of sweets, oh, last-minute plans!

Golden glow from candlelight,
Yet I’m pretty sure that’s fright.
What surprises lie in jest?
With laughter, it's the very best!

The Song of Joyful Hearts

Oh, the carols gone off-key,
Bells are ringing merrily!
Every hiccup, every squeak,
Makes the laughter last all week!

Wrap the gaffes in jolly cheer,
Rumor says that Santa's near!
Presentation falls on the floor,
But the joy? It’s worth much more!

Grandma’s sweater, loud and bright,
Makes the kittens take a fright.
Merry chaos, wrapped in love,
Filling hearts with warmth above.

From the goodies to the fun,
We'll keep laughing 'til we’re done.
Gather 'round and sing out loud,
Joyful hearts, we’re feeling proud!

Frosted Wishes on Silver Wings

Snowflakes tickle my cold nose,
A mouse in a scarf, oh how it goes!
These reindeer are late, stuck in the snow,
Can they fly? They’re moving slow!

Gingerbread men start to dance,
Spreading sugar dreams, take a chance!
Cookies in hand, what a delightful sight,
They’ve hidden the eggnog, oh what a plight!

Twinkling lights wink from every tree,
Santa's stuck in a chimney, oh me, oh my!
Elf on the shelf is plotting his prank,
Jingle bell rock is played on a tank!

Mistletoe mishaps, laughter erupts,
A cat in a hat and the dog’s interrupt!
Frosty the snowman’s melting away,
Let’s grab some cocoa, it’s time to play!

Echoes of Joy in Every Glow

Laughter echoes, round and round,
A squirrel steals the last candy found.
Tinsel tangled in my hair so bright,
I'm like a disco ball, what a sight!

Ornaments bouncing on every shelf,
Uncle Joe dancing, being himself.
Fighting for cookies, what a tough race,
I'll hide in the pantry for some more space!

The carolers sing off-key all night,
As grandpa snore-laughs, a comical sight.
With lights that flicker and sometimes blink,
We laugh till we're merry, more than you think!

Wrapping up presents with way too much tape,
It's a gift for the cat! What an escape!
From snowball fights to hot cocoa spills,
The echoes of joy give endless thrills!

Secrets of the Winter Solstice

The sun takes a nap, it’s wintertime,
Snowmen gossip and sneak a rhyme.
Chocolates are melting on everyone’s lap,
Let’s dig for the gifts; oh, what a trap!

Inside hats there’s a partridge, so sly,
A surprise for you and a pie in the eye!
Grandma’s fruitcake? It’s quite a tale,
At least the dog likes it; he’s wagging his tail!

Twinkling shadows play on the walls,
Elves stealing cookies, hear the call!
Dancing reindeer on the rooftop glide,
Shh, they’re sneaking off; let’s go for a ride!

The secrets unfold, in the snow, so bright,
Laughter and joy wrapping the night.
With every twinkling star above,
We share silly memories, wrapped in love!

Radiance Wrapped in Tinsel Ties

Bells ring loudly, a comical chime,
As I trip on tinsel, oh, what a crime!
Lights that dazzle, but they're set to strife,
I'm wrapped up like a gift for the rest of my life!

The tree starts to sway with a giggle and dance,
Even the cat thinks he's got a chance.
Presents piled high, but what's in this box?
Perhaps a pet rock—oh heck, or some socks!

Eggnog spills as we start to cheer,
A jump in the chair, don't spill the beer!
Grandpa's retelling the joke from last year,
But we roll on the floor, filled with good cheer!

With hugs and with laughter, we gather so tight,
In tinsel and ribbons, it all feels so right.
Merry and bright, with a wink in our eyes,
This holiday season brings endless surprise!

Spirit of Giving in Every Beam

Gifts wrapped tight, a cat's new game,
Tinsel flying, what a name!
Uncle Joe swipes the last sweet pie,
We all sit back and laugh and sigh.

Snowmen dance, wearing socks as hats,
Cookies vanish, where are the rats?
Giggles echo around the room,
As we munch on candy canes with gloom.

Invisible reindeer land on the floor,
Dad’s prank gifts leave us begging for more!
The tree’s adorned with mismatched flair,
Each bulb a tale, a laugh to share.

At this feast of weird delight,
Merry chaos feels just right!
With every chuckle, every cheer,
The spirit of giving draws us near.

Hearts Aglow with Evergreen Memories

Grandma's sweater, five sizes too wide,
Pine-scented hugs, a jolly ride!
Children sneaking a peek for toys,
While dancing dads make silly noise.

Lights in colors far too bright,
Twinkling bulbs shine through the night.
Oh, the reindeer that prance and play,
With mischief in every holiday sway.

Vet's dog dressed as jolly St. Nick,
Chasing dreams with a playful flick.
Every ornament holds a tiny tale,
As laughter jingles like merry bells.

Through these moments, we'll always cheer,
With hearts aglow, we hold them dear!
In a blur of joy, we find our bliss,
Wrapped in love and holiday kiss.

Luminous Tales by the Tree

Underneath that crooked tree,
A squirrel notes our glee,
With cookies stolen, and milk gone,
Jokes fly as we bond till dawn.

Flickering lights tell stories bright,
About grandpas lost in the night.
A turkey dances, what a sight,
As laughter fills the festive night.

Ornaments lost from last year’s spree,
Unbeatable treasures filled with glee.
Labels written, 'don’t eat this,'
Each gift a chorus, a merry twist.

So gather ‘round, it’s time to share,
This field of tales beyond compare.
Where every chuckle spins delight,
In luminous tales by the tree tonight.

Frosty Breath and Flickering Lights

Frosty breath escapes my lips,
As snowflakes dance, and we take trips.
A snowball fights sends us into fits,
With laughter echoing through the bits.

Flickering lights, all tangled tight,
As dad swears, this year's a fright!
The puppy chews the ribbon bold,
And finds a present, if truth be told.

Jumpers stretched like elastic bands,
In silly poses, we strike our stands.
Mistletoe hangs, but all we want,
Is the last cookie in the front.

So gather close, don't miss the cheer,
With frosty breath, our joy is clear.
In these moments, we hold our might,
Wrapped tight in laughs and flickering light.

Serenity Wrapped in Soft Glow

The lights are strung, oh what a sight,
A cat in the tree, now that's a fright!
Cookies are burning, whoops, my bad!
But laughter is everywhere, how can you be sad?

The wreath's upside down, a holiday fail,
Uncle Joe’s sweater, a colorful trail.
With every mishap, we giggle with glee,
Together we shine, like the lights on the tree.

Threads of Gold in the Silver Night

The snowflakes fall, like fluff on a cake,
While Dad's in the kitchen, making a mistake.
He says 'just a dash' but spills half the spice,
Mom's rolling her eyes, 'Oh, isn't this nice?'

Gifts wrapped in paper, stuck with a bow,
One’s from the cat, who knew it was show.
We gather around for the tales of the past,
While giggles erupt, oh how they will last.

Dancing Flames in a Peaceful Hearth

The fire's crackling, a warm little glow,
A marshmallow's crying, it's losing the show.
Grandma is singing, off-key but sincere,
While we all pretend we can't really hear!

The stockings are hung, but wait, who is this?
A squirrel sneaks in for a nutty bliss.
We laugh as we tell tales, both silly and bright,
In the cozy chaos of this merry night.

Mirthful Carols Under the Sky

Carolers gather, all off a bit pitch,
Mom joins in loudly, in her holiday stitch.
The neighbor's dog howls, joining the beat,
While we share our cookies, oh what a treat!

With each silly dance, we stomp in delight,
And snowballs are flying from left and from right.
Under the stars, what a whimsical sight,
A season of joy, silly, merry, and bright!

Delight of Festive Dreams

Twinkling lights on every tree,
Even my cat thinks it's a party!
Cookies stacked high, oh what a sight,
Must taste them all, it feels so right.

Snowflakes falling with a cheer,
Uncle Joe's dance—oh dear, oh dear!
Grandma's got her holiday cheer,
Watch out for her fruitcake, my dear!

Reindeer games in the front yard,
Mittens lost, it's getting hard!
Sledding down the slope so fast,
Laughter echoes, what a blast!

Presents wrapped and piled high,
Who needs a gift? Just pass me pie!
Under the mistletoe we stand,
Oops! A kiss, not what I planned!

Wedding of Light and Silence

Candles flicker in the night,
Grandpa's snoring—a funny sight!
Lights are tangled, oh what a feat,
Even the dog thinks it's a treat.

Jingle bells ring out with glee,
Mom's out dancing, just wait and see!
Socks on the cat—now that's a look,
Who knew Christmas was in a book?

Snowmen stacked with silly hats,
Barking with laughter, all our chats.
Hot cocoa spills on the floor,
Oops! Just part of the holiday lore.

Under mistletoe, a shy glance,
Who knew my crush would breakdance?
Laughter mingles with the cheer,
Christmas time, we hold so dear!

The Promise of Tomorrow's Joy

Stockings hung with hopes galore,
Mom says there's food—let's eat more!
The turkey's dancing on the plate,
Wait! Someone's trying to imitate!

Jolly old Santa with a wink,
His beard's stuck in my drink!
Reindeer flying through the air,
Land, my friends, without a care!

Gifts wrapped tight, what's inside?
A sweater two sizes wide!
Grandma giggles, what a sight,
Turns out it's her secret delight.

Laughter rings from every room,
Why does the tree still smell like gloom?
Tomorrow brings its shiny bling,
But first, another holiday fling!

Beneath the Evergreen's Embrace

Underneath the tree so bright,
Uncle Fred is lost tonight!
Wrapped in lights, what a surprise,
Not for me, but for the pies!

Snowflakes land on my hot cocoa,
Now it’s a chilly fashion show!
Tinsel twirls around my hat,
Who knew festive meant falling flat?

Cookies made in a funny shape,
Santa's diet, please escape!
Silly hats on my siblings' heads,
Looks like we’re all going to bed!

Joyful laughter fills the air,
An ornament stuck in my hair!
Beneath the branches, visions dwell,
In cozy chaos, all is well!

The Dance of Colors in the Snow

A red squirrel prances with grace,
Wearing a hat, what a curious case!
Frosty the snowman, with a carrot nose,
Wobbles and jigs, as everyone knows.

The trees wear garlands, a style so bright,
Even the raccoons join in the light!
Snowflakes giggle as they twirl and fall,
Painting the world for one and for all.

Neighbors peek out from their cozy retreats,
Wishing for cocoa and sugar-rolled treats!
The wind plays a tune, a jovial sound,
As laughter echoes all around.

With every jump and jolly little slide,
Joy spills over, there's much to provide!
In the dance of colors, we jump and sway,
Winter's a party, hip-hip-hooray!

Lanterns of Laughter and Love

In every window, a candle glows,
The cat flips the switch and oh, how it shows!
Stripes of bright colors, a circus delight,
Who knew a kitten could be such a fright?

The cookies are baking, the dough's on the floor,
The dog sneaks a nibble, just one little score.
Grandma's on skates, what a hilarious sight,
Spinning like stars 'neath the shimmering light.

Jingle bells jangle, the tune goes askew,
As unicycles roll through the frosty blue.
With giggles and grins, our hearts start to soar,
The joy of the season is hard to ignore!

So let's fill our lanterns with laughter and cheer,
And shine bright with love, as the season draws near.
For laughter is magic, it flows and it twirls,
In the dance of joy, let's give it a whirl!

Ember Threads of Memory's Thread

The fireplace crackles, as stories unfold,
A dragon once lived, or so I am told.
Grandpa insists he was friends with that beast,
While we try hard not to laugh 'til we feast.

Each ember a memory, glowing so bright,
With visions of cousins and snowball fight night.
A tussle ensues, the snowballs fly fast,
We'll treasure these moments, both present and past!

The cat in a stocking, what a silly sight,
Chasing after shadows, into the black night.
Tickles and giggles fill up the grand room,
As we bask in the warmth, the memories bloom.

So raise up a glass to the laughs and the gleam,
The tales that grow taller with each silly theme.
In ember threads woven, our hearts feel so light,
Embracing the joy as we sing with delight!

Night's Cloak Adorned in Light

The moon wears a halo, it's quite the grand piece,
As lights twinkle softly, inviting sweet peace.
The raccoons are plotting their holiday heist,
In search of the cookies, they're ready to feast!

With candy cane stripes, the kids start to dance,
Pretending they're reindeer, giving it a chance.
Tinsel gets tangled, what a sight to behold,
As laughter erupts in a chorus of gold.

The stars are like sprinkles on dark velvet skies,
While elves do a jig, sharing giggles and sighs.
With snowflakes in hand and mismatched socks bright,
We embrace the adventure, this wonderful night.

So gather together, let humor take flight,
As we dream in the magic of laughter's own light.
For night's cloak adorned, we sing loud and clear,
Making memories together, year after year!

A Tapestry of Light and Shadow

The bulbs are blinking, what a sight,
My cat's in a tangle, oh what a fright!
Twinkling stars dance on our roof,
While Uncle Joe's tripped, that's the proof!

A Santa in shades struts down the street,
With candy cane socks on his feet.
The tree's leaning wildly to one side,
As if it's trying to enjoy the ride!

Grandma's baking cookies, what bliss,
But waits for the kids, to taste and miss.
Frosting on noses, giggles so bright,
Sugar rush turning kids into flight!

Jingle bells ringing, it's time to cheer,
But who stole the eggnog? Oh dear, oh dear!
We laugh as we scurry, no moment to cease,
In this mad little world, our chaos is peace!

Glistening Paths to Comfort and Cheer

The snowflakes flutter like butterflies,
While Dad's stuck on the roof, what a surprise!
Icicles hang like a jolly old grin,
As we search for the ornaments, where have they been?

Sisters squabble over who gets to choose,
The color of lights, why do they confuse?
Mom's on the couch with a book and a drink,
While we untangle lights, making us rethink!

The cocoa's bubbling, but wait, what's that?
A marshmallow avalanche, oh dear, oh rat!
Laughter erupts, it's a sweet silly fight,
Hot chocolate madness, what pure delight!

With reindeer jokes flying around the room,
And knitted sweaters that challenge the plume,
We revel in warmth, through giggles and cheer,
In the light of our joy, the season is here!

Fragments of Joy in the Frost

Frosty the snowman is ready to play,
As the kids roll their snowballs all day.
A carrot for a nose, a hat on his head,
While the snowflakes giggle, "Let's go, let's spread!"

The dogs are barking, chasing their tails,
While Santa's lost in our snowy trails.
With a ho ho ho, and a slip on the ice,
He waves with delight, oh isn't it nice?

The fireplace crackles, popcorn to pop,
And cards of bad puns make our laughter nonstop.
Rudolph's red nose is a beacon so bright,
Leading us home through the wild winter night!

Pine needles tickle, with scents oh so sweet,
While decorum dashes right off of our feet.
In a whirl of joy, we toast with our cheer,
In the glow of the fun, this season is dear!

Echoes of Carols Through the Night

Carols are sung with a twist in the tune,
As Cousin Tim dances like a cartoon.
The tree tips and wobbles, oh watch out now,
As the cat makes a leap, holy cow!

The cookies are burnt, should we order out?
With icing disasters, there's laughter, no doubt.
A garland above, it's a serious art,
But the dog thinks it's food, oh bless his heart!

Sipping hot cider, warm and so snug,
Uncle Dave's telling tales of a bug.
Every joke comes with a punchline in sight,
As we share in the laughter, oh what a night!

The snow gently falls, a calming refrain,
While the chaos of Christmas wraps us in gain.
With giggles and joy echoing around,
In the spirit of fun, true magic is found!

Enchanted Evenings Under the Christmas Sky

Snowmen dance, with carrot noses bright,
They twirl and giggle, under the night light.
Elves drop cookies—who knew they'd bring cheer?
Santa’s on a treadmill, avoiding the beer!

Twinkling lights flicker, they wink and tease,
Frosty steals cocoa, he’s playing with ease.
Christmas trees whisper, they hunt for a snack,
While the cat’s in the garland, on the attack!

Threads of Silver in Starry Spaces

Singing carols, the neighbors look on,
Raccoons in hats, as dawn turns to dawn.
With mistletoe traps, they lure in the fam,
But Auntie just slipped - wearing her best jam!

Jingle bells jangle, a wintry parade,
While kids laugh and chuckle, in snow they cascade.
Gifts wrapped in mayhem, what's hiding inside?
An onion? A sock? Surprises won't hide!

Glows of Gratitude in Soft Reflect

Cookies fresh baked, but crumbs all around,
Rats in tuxedos are dancing—profound!
With ribbons a-flying, kids swing with delight,
A dog joins the chaos, he thinks it's a fight!

Hot cocoa splashes, whipped cream on their nose,
Each sip is a giggle, as sweetness just flows.
Grandma's fruitcake? It's now a doorstop!
But we hold it dear; oh, the laughs never stop!

A Truce with Winter's Chill

Winter arrives with a grin and a scoff,
But snowflakes are melting; they're thin like a cloth.
Sledding down hills, we fly like a kite,
Hoping we land in a snowdrift, just right!

Winter wonders why we wear socks so thick,
When we're stuck in the snow, we do the ol' slick.
With laughter and warmth, we gather 'round tight,
The season is silly, it's pure delight!

Snowflakes and Starlight Whispers

Snowflakes tumble, a wintery dance,
Squirrels in hats take every chance.
They slip and slide on frosty ground,
Chasing their tails, round and round.

Pine trees dressed in sparkly cheer,
Giggling ornaments all draw near.
A snowman winks with a carrot nose,
Trying on shades, striking a pose.

Children bundled up, fingers numb,
Make snowballs that go 'thwump!' not 'thrum.'
Laughter erupts as they throw and duck,
Oops! Now mom's got to clean that muck!

The moonlight giggles, the night is bright,
As penguins slide, what a silly sight!
With fluffy pillows and dreams that soar,
The magic of winter keeps us wanting more!

The Symphony of Brightened Nights

Choruses of laughter fill the air,
Gingerbread men are dancing everywhere.
A cat in a scarf chases a mouse,
While grandma mixes up beer with the house.

Jingle bells jangle, tunes gone absurd,
Fido sings loudly, oh how he's heard!
The tree sways gently, the star's a bit drunk,
Hoping to find out who's made this funk.

Mistakes in the cookie, a colorful mess,
Sprinkles on faces, we all must confess.
Sipping hot cocoa, with marshmallows spry,
Spiked with some joy, oh my, oh my!

The wrapping paper's now a playground,
People trip over it, giggling sound.
With drums made of pots and laughter so bright,
What a delightful and wacky night!

A Candle's Flame in the Winter Bliss

Candles flicker with tales to tell,
One lights another, and oh what a spell!
The cat’s on the table, he thinks he can sing,
While grandpa insists he was once a king.

Marshmallows pop in a hot, bubbling pot,
'These are gourmet!' declares a chef not.
The kitchen's aroma, a chaotic delight,
As flour flies high—a soft powdery fight.

Scarves all tangled from a joyful embrace,
Mom's mistletoe plan has gone quite out of place.
So many presents, we can barely fit,
But who wrapped the socks? It’s still a great hit!

A toast with a wink, as stories unfold,
Of Christmas disasters we happened to hold.
With smiles all around, and warmth in our hearts,
The simple joys turn into perfect arts!

Shimmering Tales of the Holiday Night

Twinkling lights like mischievous fairies,
Nestled on rooftops, still so very scary.
Inflatable Santa starts to deflate,
Rolling around like he's lost his fate.

Snowmen declare their snowball fights loud,
While kids join in, feeling so proud.
A puppy's head pops from a bright red sack,
Barking, "I'm part of the festive pack!"

Gifts wrapped in colors that clash and collide,
Neighbors all wonder what's had us bide.
A tinsel tornado, what a wild sight,
All in the spirit, laughing with delight!

The stars overhead seem to crack silly jokes,
As we share our stories, laughter provokes.
With cheer in the air, we dance through the night,
Making crazy memories, oh what a delight!

Kindred Spirits in the Winter's Glow

Snowflakes dance on a chocolate cake,
Reindeer prance while the cookies bake.
Santa's lost in the jingle bell jam,
But hey, who needs a merry old man?

Gifts are wrapped in last year's news,
With bows made from leftover shoes.
Elves giggle, trying to sneak a peek,
At the gifts that are looking quite bleak.

Mischief thrives in the cozy light,
As snowmen argue who’s wrong or right.
Hot cocoa spills, and laughter grows,
They stumble through snow, like flashy pros.

In this season of whimsy and cheer,
We sip on punch while spinning in fear.
For next year’s diet begins on the day,
A funny dance of the holiday sway.

Fables of Frost and Warmth

Frosty mornings bring giggles and grins,
As kids throw snowballs, seeking their wins.
Sledding down hills, a comical sight,
While warm mittens vanish, it's pure delight.

Chilly cats snooze by the fire's embrace,
With twinkly lights all over the place.
Grandma's secret eggnog, a wild ride,
Sipping too much, and we just might glide.

Bells clang loudly, a jolly refrain,
As relatives gather, it's always the same.
Old uncle's jokes make the table shake,
And auntie's casserole? A big mistake!

Under the mistletoe, a caper ensues,
A clumsy dance, oh what a ruse!
With laughter ringing, the fun does ignite,
In tales of joy and silly delight.

Reflections in the Windowpane

The reflections sparkle, oh what a show,
As snowmen plot with a wink and a glow.
Candy canes twist in a comical fight,
While gingerbread cookies lose all their bite.

Mice in the pantry, a festive brigade,
Nibbling on treats that we should have saved.
The cat sits watching with glee in its eye,
While dreams of sugarplums waltz by and by.

Frost on the glass tells stories so sweet,
Of hidden presents and holidays neat.
Pine scent wafts in with a playful cheer,
As giggles and snorts fill the chilly air.

Each windowpane holds a tale to be told,
Of clashing colors, and memories bold.
With cheeks all rosy, we toast with delight,
To the joyous mischief that is our night!

A Tapestry of Silver and Gold

With tinsel shining, the tree starts to sway,
As ornaments bounce in their festive ballet.
Uncle Bob slips, and we all burst in laughs,
His pants caught in pine, oh how time half-passed!

Garlands of laughter drape over the chairs,
While playful whispers fill the frosty airs.
Secret Santa’s gift is a cat in a box,
Who thought wrapping pets was a clever paradox?

Mugs full of cocoa, marshmallows afloat,
Holiday music in a comical note.
A salute with the punch, a toast to the scene,
As we jingle and jangle like no one’s ever seen.

Under glittering skies, we dance and we dash,
Sharing thoughts of the year and a holiday splash.
In a tapestry woven from laughter so sweet,
We celebrate joy—now let's all take a seat!

The Firelight of Hopeful Hearts

The logs are stacked, so tall and proud,
A dance of flames draws in the crowd.
Marshmallows roast with a hearty cheer,
But the smoke makes Grandma disappear!

The kids all shout, 'It's snowing white!'
Just as dad slips, what a funny sight!
He tumbles down with a startled yelp,
Makes us all laugh, can't help ourselves!

A cat in a hat, what a strange view,
Purring by the fire, feeling brand new.
With laughter echoing throughout the night,
We warm our hearts in the flickering light.

So gather around this joyous blaze,
With s'mores and stories, let's set the phase.
For in this warmth, we find our glee,
A whimsical night, just you and me!

Radiant Moments in Winter's Caress

Outside the snow creates a show,
While hot cocoa's steaming, just so you know.
Sipping too fast, oh what a mistake,
A face like a lobster, for goodness' sake!

We venture out in bundled attire,
Just to fall over, that's our desire.
Snowballs are flying, giggles abound,
But watch out for snowmen, they stand their ground!

The dog goes wild in snowy delight,
Chasing his shadow, with all his might.
He skids on the ice, what a clumsy pup,
We can't help but laugh, oh come join us up!

Under twinkling lights, we revel and sing,
With cookie crumbs stuck on everything.
Our hearts full of joy, as we make a toast,
To radiant moments we cherish the most!

Threads of Wonder in the Chill

A scarf wrapped tightly, oh what a fright,
Can't feel my nose, is that a good sight?
Shoveling snow, I slip and glide,
And now my insurance is on my side!

The ornaments twinkle like stars in space,
While Uncle Joe tries to shuffle with grace.
His dance is wild, he trips on the rug,
But laughter erupts; he's a dancing bug!

Baking cookies, who knew it’s an art?
Flour fights break out, floury mayhem's smart.
Sprinkle disasters cover the floor,
But oh we will laugh; it’s what we adore!

So wrap me in warmth, and pass the pie,
With tidings of joy that will surely fly.
As threads of laughter weave through the chill,
We celebrate moments, we love them still!

Eternal Glow of Winter's Embrace

In the frosty air, we build a big fort,
Only to find someone brought the dessert!
With gingerbread houses, a sticky fight,
Now frosting's dripping; what a funny sight!

The carolers sing outside my door,
One falls in the snow, two laugh at the score.
With voices raised, we join in parade,
Doing our best, but choreography's delayed!

A hot fire crackles, bringing us close,
But mom dropped the logs, so we roast the toast!
We snicker and munch, laughter fills the air,
With hearts glowing bright, no problems to bear.

So here’s to the season filled with mishaps,
Where joy and laughter earn all the claps.
In every moment we find delight,
In this silly season, our spirits take flight!

Echoes of Togetherness in Winter's Embrace

Snowflakes fall like whispered cheer,
We gather 'round, not a single sneer.
Gather the snacks, the cocoa's hot,
Laughter erupts—oh, it's quite the plot!

Grandma's stories, they twist and twine,
Mixing up truths with a dash of wine.
Uncle Joe's dance—a sight to see,
His moves are wild, but we let it be.

Chasing kids through a frozen maze,
Hilarity reigns in our festive haze.
A snowman made of leftover pie,
We giggle and gasp as it starts to fly!

With mittens lost and scarves askew,
We all look like hedgehogs, it's truly true.
Yet here we are, all snug and bright,
Embracing joy, our hearts take flight.

A Dance of Lights in the Evening's Calm

Twinkling bulbs on a crazy spree,
Blinky, winky—now they're free!
Little Timmy's fingers, quite a sight,
He trips and falls—oh, what a fright!

The cat's on the tree, hanging by a thread,
Dancing to music in her fluffy head.
Fairy lights tangled, a kitty's delight,
As we laugh and strive to make it right.

Our neighbor's show is too much to bear,
Lasers and fireworks fizzle in the air.
With popcorn guns and hotdog fights,
We cheer while sipping hot cocoa bites.

Yet here we stand, with mismatched cheer,
Swaying together, with hugs so near.
In this crazy bash, 'tis quite alright,
For laughter lingers in every light.

Wishes Floating on the Winter Breeze

The mailman’s lost with our wish list here,
Christmas cards stuck, it's really unclear.
A reindeer’s picked up our flying mail,
But instead it’s got gum—oh, what a fail!

Snowmen smile with carrot noses,
Telling witty jokes that nobody knows.
Each wish we share whispers through the night,
Though it's just a squirrel clutching a bite.

The wind carries chuckles above the trees,
As snowflakes dance like a winter breeze.
What we ask for is always a treat,
A tree full of cookies—now that's hard to beat!

In the night’s hush, we dream and confide,
With giggles and gabs, we take it in stride.
Wishes written in candy cane ink,
Floating together, in laughter, we sink.

The Art of Giving in Silent Nights

Presents wrapped with tape gone wild,
A trail of paper left by a child.
Inside a box, a sock, maybe two,
Guess what? It’s mine, but looks good on you!

Silent nights, with sneaky surprises,
Grandpa's gift—a pair of weird disguises.
Tangled lights? Oh what a mess,
But we wear them proudly, no need to impress.

Cookies and sprinkles, all a bit crumby,
The icing's a riot; it makes me feel grumpy.
But smiles are the magic we gift in delight,
Unruly and joyous on this silly night.

As we toast with cider and laugh a bit hard,
Mom’s gotten stuck inside the gift card.
In the spirit of giving, we twirl and we tread,
For laughter and joy are the gifts we spread.

Embracing the Spirit of Giving

Santa's sleigh is stuck in traffic,
Reindeer take a coffee break.
Elves try to wrap gifts in a hurry,
But tangled lights make them irate.

We gifted socks to Uncle Fred,
He wears them on his hands instead.
Grandma's baking cookies late,
Hope she doesn't burn the plate!

The cat climbs high on the decor,
Swatting ornaments off the floor.
Kids laugh loud, they sing off-key,
Joyful chaos, let it be!

Wrapping paper's strewn about,
Some gifts we forgot to shout.
With fun and cheer, we'll persevere,
Another year, full of good cheer!

Luminescence of the Season's Heart

Twinkling lights are a big hit,
Somehow we made a great big split.
The lawn’s a mess, with Santa’s sleigh,
But neighbors laugh it off, hooray!

Gingerbread houses lean to one side,
Candy canes act like a slide.
Kids go wild, they stomp and cheer,
It's the silliest time of the year!

A snowman’s hat flies in the air,
Kids chase it with frantic flair.
Sledding down a hill of snow,
And face-first in the yard they go!

Mistletoe hung just way too low,
A kiss on the cheek, then off they go.
With laughter, cheer, and holiday jests,
We celebrate with all our guests!

Shadows Dancing by the Fire

By the fire, we roast marshmallows,
But overheated, they turn to jellos.
We joke and laugh, no plans to tire,
As shadows dance and hopes conspire.

Hot cocoa spills on Grandma's lap,
She promptly falls into a nap.
Kids steal cookies from the tray,
While squirrels watch from far away.

Dad’s stuck in his reindeer suit,
Squeezing through the door, he does a hoot.
A dance-off breaks; who will rehearse?
Mom twirls in her edible purse!

With every cheer and slightly burnt pie,
We share our joy and watch the sky.
Each shadow whispers tales of fun,
As the merry night is never done!

The Magic of Starlit Celebrations

Under starlit skies, we gather tight,
And wonder how to get the lights right.
A ladder tips, Dad takes a dive,
"Next time we'll just not try!" we jive.

Cousins hide gifts behind the tree,
Then forget where they hid them, oh me!
The dog thinks it's a new chew toy,
Now presents come minus some joy.

The punch bowl has too much 'zazz',
A clumsy sip, and it's a razz.
With hiccuped giggles, we spill our glee,
Making memories, oh so free!

Yet still we laugh through every cheer,
As the starlight twinkles ever near.
With joy and love, we dance and play,
Creating magic in a funny way!